HOW TO
Keep Your
Church
Out of
Court

Stephen P. Chawaga

CPH.
SAINT LOUIS

To my wife, Laurie

Contents

Preface

Jesus said, "Give to Caesar what is Caesar's, and to God what is God's" (Matthew 22:21). And again, "My kingdom is not of this world" (John 18:36). From these words and others we find that Scripture makes a distinction between two kingdoms—the kingdom of God and the kingdom of this world. Both kingdoms are under the rule of God, but in different ways.

The kingdom of God is a kingdom of grace. Its visible expression in this world is the church of Jesus Christ. In this kingdom God forgives sins and grants eternal life to all who repent of their sins and believe in His Son, Jesus Christ. God does this on the basis of the holy, innocent suffering and death of Christ on the cross of Calvary and the glorious resurrection of Christ from the dead. In this kingdom God delivers grace through means: the Word of God and the sacraments of Baptism and Holy Communion. Thus, the kingdom of God is the kingdom of God's right hand, as it were. In His right hand He holds a chalice, the cup of forgiveness that is ours in the blood of Christ.

The kingdom of this world is a kingdom of force. Its visible expression in this world is the state. In this kingdom God punishes criminals, provides for the common defense, and establishes civil order. God does this on the basis of His sovereignty as maker of heaven and earth. In this kingdom God exercises force through means: the civil authorities. "The authorities that exist have been established by God" (Romans 13:1). Thus, the kingdom of this world is the kingdom of God's left hand. In His left hand He holds a sword, the symbol of secular power.

As Christians, we are members of both kingdoms. As members of the church, we attend services to hear the Word of God proclaimed and to receive the Sacraments for the strengthening of our faith. As citizens of the state, we pay our taxes, obey the laws of the land, and serve in the military when required. In an ideal world, church and state would each operate in their respective spheres and not intrude upon the prerogatives of the other.

Unfortunately, such is not always the case. During the Middle Ages in Europe, the church wielded secular authority to a great extent, and the popes held dominion over kings. During the twentieth century, atheistic states such as the Soviet Union tried to destroy the church. In both cases, the results were disastrous for the common people. In America today, we live in a highly litigious society. People are quick to sue over real or imagined injustices or injuries. While the government is not trying to destroy the church, it is often called upon to settle disputes over church property and personnel

6

issues. The results of a lawsuit can be disastrous for the ordinary members of a local congregation.

We certainly want to keep our church out of court if at all possible. This book will show how in a simple way. Pastors, church officers, trustees, treasurers, and all leaders and laity will want to consult the suggestions here offered, in the interest of better stewardship over the resources God has entrusted to our care.

Introduction

L ook around your church's neighborhood. Whether it is located in an urban or rural setting, or somewhere in between, it is probably a focal point for the community. Your church almost certainly commands a significant amount of property. The space you inhabit represents the commitment of your church's founders to your community and to God. To be faithful stewards of this obligation, you and the other members of your congregation should pledge to maintain as responsibly as you can your property and the environment in which you meet and work.

Ensuring that your premises are safe for visitors is one aspect of this commitment. Your parishioners are entitled to expect that they can worship in a nurturing environment, and your neighbors and the public should be able to pass through your property in peace. Just as significantly, however, your employees and volunteers have a right to expect a pleasant work environment and that they will be treated fairly and with respect. Understanding the risks that affect these expectations is the first step in preventing them. This book will assist you in determining how to treat your parishioners, employees, and neighbors with the care the law requires of you. While no one can guarantee that your church will never face a lawsuit, you can minimize the chances of having to defend against, or pay money as the result of, a claim of negligence or intentional misconduct that has led to an injury by applying the basic principles set out in the following pages.

1

General Principles
of Liability

You may be required to compensate someone who is injured while on your church premises if he or she establishes that you failed to do something you could have done to keep the property safe. How much you have to do to prevent an accident depends, in part, on whom you are protecting.

A person who enters your property or buildings can be characterized as a trespasser, licensee, or invitee. A trespasser is someone who is on your property without your permission. A licensee is someone you have authorized to enter onto your premises for a particular purpose, either expressly or by implication, but who has no reason to think you have taken special precautions for his safety. An invitee, by contrast, is someone you have specifically invited onto your property for a social or a business reason, and who therefore is entitled to believe that you are looking out for her.

For many years, judges and juries have used this classification system as a means for determining the level of care owners of premises owe to various people. To trespassers, only the lowest duty is owed. The level of obligation rises for licensees, and it is even higher for those you invite onto your property. While some courts do not hold strictly to these categories, almost all will look to the relationship between you as the property owner and the person bringing the claim against you to determine whether you failed to meet your duty of care to that person. Accordingly, if you understand these classifications, you can figure out what you need to do on your property to keep your visitors safe.

Liability to Trespassers

You don't have to do much to keep your premises safe for trespassers, as they shouldn't be on your property to begin with. However, you may not intentionally try to inflict bodily harm upon them, such as by setting a hidden trap, if you have not exercised reasonable care to warn of the possible risk. Thus, if you put a fence topped with barbed wire around your church cemetery and don't post large, prominent signs warning people of this fact, you could be liable to a vandal who is injured while climbing the fence. If you leave off the barbed wire, however, you are probably not liable to a trespasser who is hurt in a fall from the top of the fence, since you did not hide any dangers from that person.

If you know a particular person is trespassing on your property, you then have to take some additional precautions to protect his or her safety. This may be a challenge if you view the trespasser as an actual threat to your property and its contents. Remember, however, that a trespasser can also include someone as innocent as a neighbor who cuts through your property on a shortcut to her home, or a schoolchild playing in a neighboring field who runs onto your driveway to retrieve a basketball. The law requires you to be aware of conditions on your property and to take reasonable precautions to protect the safety of anyone you know might be on it, whether with your consent or not. Thus, if you know that a person is sleeping in your sanctuary during hours when it is closed to the public, you may be liable to him if he is injured by falling plaster from your church's ceiling if you were aware that the ceiling needed repair.

You should also bear in mind that the law imposes a special duty upon property owners to protect trespassing children. Children are given certain allowances for their youthful exuberance, and you have a duty to use reasonable care to keep them safe from conditions against which you might expect them to be unable to protect themselves. If there is something dangerous on your property and you know both that it could cause a child serious bodily harm and that a child, because of his or her age, would not appreciate this risk, you must take reasonable care to either eliminate the danger or protect children that might encounter it. This rule is often called the "doctrine of attractive nuisance," because it applies to things on your property that are problems for you but alluring to children as play items.

One example is a crumbling stone wall that you might find on your grounds. If you know that children from the neighborhood like to enter your property and use the wall as a play fortress, and if one is injured when some stones fall on her while she is lying at the base of the wall, you may be subject to liability to that child because it would have been easy for you to either repair or dismantle the wall. You would not be liable, however, if the children had frequently seen stones come loose from the wall during the course of their play and had mentioned this fact to someone in authority, for then it would be clear that they were as aware as any adult that the wall was crumbling.

Your duty to trespassing children does not extend, therefore, to conditions that are obvious even to them—like a pond where they might drown if they swim in it or a roof from which they might fall if they climb it. Nor are you required to childproof your property against all potential hazards. As one court noted in concluding that a church was not liable for the injuries suffered by a Sunday school student who fell into a light well,

> there is almost no condition which an adventurous child cannot turn into an injury-producer: trees, swings, slides, stairs, hard-surfaced playgrounds, and soft-surfaced playgrounds can all be a source of harm to the young. ... Only when a jury might find that the risk to children is unreasonable and that the harm possible is serious is there a question of fact to be determined. (*Sum-*

mers v Grant Park Baptist Church, 243 Ore 362, 364
[Ore 1966])

You should not assume, however, that all courts will give you the benefit of the doubt, and as a prudent parish you should err well on the side of caution in dealing with potential hazards to children.

Liability to Licensees

If you have given permission to someone to be on your premises, that person is not a trespasser but is referred to as a "licensee." Your consent can either be express, such as when a softball team asks to use an undeveloped portion of your property as a practice field and you agree, or implied by your failure to object to the person's presence. Just because you do not take steps to remove a trespasser from your property, however, does not in and of itself make the trespasser a licensee; the facts of the specific case must be looked at to determine whether you can fairly be said to have consented to his or her remaining on your premises.

You are liable to licensees for dangers that you know exist on your property but that they do not. You are not obliged to eliminate such risks from your property, but you must warn licensees about them. You do not have to inspect your premises to discover potential dangers, or do anything to prepare for a licensee's visit. For example, if you allow a member of a neighboring church onto your property to attend an evening meeting and you know your driveway has a large pothole that can't be seen at night, you may have a duty to warn this member of the pothole's existence. You would not have the same duty if the meeting takes place during the day, when the pothole would be plainly visible to the licensee, or if the pothole was not created until the day of the meeting and you couldn't reasonably be expected to have become aware of it.

A warning sign, prominently posted and disclosing the danger, is likely to satisfy your duty to licensees. In the example of the pothole, for instance, an illuminated notice displayed at the entrance to your driveway that says "WARNING: POTHOLE AHEAD" is probably satisfactory. A more generic signal to "BE CAREFUL," by contrast, probably will not suffice.

Liability to Invitees

In the case of certain people who come onto your premises, you not only consent to their entry on your land, you actually desire them to come. The classic example is a store owner's relationship with his or her customers; the owner not only tolerates patrons, he or she actively solicits them. Such people are known as "invitees," and you owe them a higher duty than you do licensees because you have encouraged them to enter onto your property. Some judges view members of a congregation as licensees only, reasoning that they confer no material or commercial benefit on the church and that they are called by God, not the parish itself, to attend services. Most courts take a broader view, however, and consider parishioners to be invitees because they are specifically invited to use church property and make a financial contribution to its upkeep. One court reasoned:

> Religious bodies do expressly and impliedly invite members to come and attend their services and functions. They hold their doors open to the public. ... [C]hurches do depend on contributions much the same as historical sites do, in order that they continue to be open to the public. Therefore, a church member who does not exceed the scope of a church's invitation, is an invitee while attending a church for church services or related functions. (*Clark v Moore Memorial United Methodist Church,* 538 So2d 760, 764 [Miss 1989])

You must not only warn invitees of dangers that you know about, but you must also use reasonable care for their safety if you expect they would not realize the extent of the danger. This means that you must be on the lookout for things on your property that could cause harm and fix anything you find. Thus, your unawareness of a pothole created on the day of an evening meeting might not excuse you from liability to the attendees if a reasonable inspection by you would have uncovered it. You would still not likely be responsible, however, if the pothole caused an accident during the day, since you are not liable for dangers that are considered "open and obvious."

Before taking great comfort from this "open and obvious" protection, however, remember that what is manifestly evident to you may not be to an invitee who is elderly or disabled, and it is that person's perception that counts. A person who is blind and trips on a crack in your sidewalk may have a case against you even if the crack would have been plainly visible to a person who can see, provided she was using a cane or guide dog or otherwise taking ordinary and prudent precautions. Accordingly, you should not gear your maintenance program to only the most physically able of your potential visitors.

One of the most common accidents is a fall while in church. A parish may be liable to the parishioner if the fall was caused by some unusual condition on the floor that could have been prevented or corrected before the parishioner encountered it. Thus, for example, when church sextons waxed the center aisle one Sunday afternoon before a late service, but did not buff the floors or even take steps to remove standing puddles of wax prior to the service, a congregant slipped on the wax and was injured. He sued, and the jury concluded that the church acted negligently in not properly finishing the job it started or even posting a warning sign that the floor was slippery. The same result was reached when a parishioner fell in a church aisle on a rainy day and the ushers, when questioned, could not recall that the aisle had been mopped. Compare these cases to one where a court found that a church was not liable when a parishioner slipped in a wet aisle. In this case, the evidence showed that the congregants had tracked in the water when they arrived during a heavy rainstorm, leaving the church no opportunity to remedy the unusual condition. The lack of opportunity to correct the problem saved the church from liability.

The dangers from ice and snow are treated similarly. A church is probably not going to be held liable for failing to remove snow from steps and grounds during or immediately after a storm. Property owners typically are not held responsible for accidents to their invitees arising from slippery or icy conditions of walks or steps that are no more hazardous than the generally prevailing conditions. If, however, you make no effort to remove ice and snow or to take other appropriate corrective action within a reasonable time after the snowfall ends, you will have to pay if someone is injured on the dangerous condition you have ignored.

Distinguishing Licensees from Invitees

Telling licensees from invitees is not always easy. Typically, to be an invitee, a person must either be a member of the public asked to visit your premises for a public religious or nonreligious purpose—an organ recital, for instance—or someone who comes for a business purpose, such as a plumber who comes to fix a leaky sink. One judge noted that to determine whether a guest was a licensee or an invitee required an examination of all the reasons for the person's presence on your property, including "the nature of the visit, the motives which inspire it and the benefits which flow from it." A caterer, for example, would be an invitee even if he were catering a social event like an annual dinner, because the church contacted him and asked him to enter the premises. Your employees are usually considered invitees as well. A casual sightseer, by contrast, who peeks in while your doors are open to look at some prominent stained glass windows, is only a licensee because she was not specifically invited to enter (*Atwood v Board of Trustees of First Presbyterian Church of Caldwell*, 26 NJ Super 607, 610 [1953]).

The legal distinction between an invitee and a licensee is that you are liable to an invitee for your negligence in maintaining your premises, but not to a licensee unless you were aware of the specific condition that caused his or her injury, had the opportunity to issue a warning, and failed to do so. Suppose you have a rug at the entrance to your sanctuary on which people may slip because it lacks a rubberized bottom to grip the floor beneath. If the rug were to give way when an invitee stepped on it, causing her an injury, you could well be liable to her even if no one had fallen previously. The fact that you installed a rug that would have appeared dangerous on close inspection might be sufficient by itself to establish liability against you, whether or not you conducted such an inspection. A licensee, however, would most likely have to prove that you either conducted such an inspection or that you had actual notice of the flaw in the rug from some other means, like the fact that several other people slipped on it, before he could recover for the same injuries.

Making Your Church Safer

Many of the steps you can take to minimize the risk of an accident on your premises are simple and inexpensive. First, you should have a safety committee that meets regularly and that is in charge of minimizing the risks of injury on your premises. Some activities that would be appropriate for such a committee:

- Patrolling the grounds regularly in search of hidden and even obvious dangers that have gone unattended. The safety committee should be empowered to make short-term repairs and put up warning signs on the spot, and they should be instructed to report all defects discovered to the appropriate person within the church who is responsible for effecting a permanent solution. The committee should take special care to look after hazards like ice and snow, broken walkways, and loose trash.

- Putting together one or more first-aid kits, placing them in locations where they are likely to be used (including the kitchen and the main office), monitoring their use, and replenishing them as needed.

- Monitoring the condition of tools and work equipment owned by the church, ensuring that safety items like gloves and goggles are available to volunteers involved in any building or maintenance projects, and repairing or replacing ladders, power tools, and other items as they become worn.

- Inspecting kitchen equipment regularly for electrical and other problems, maintaining working fire extinguishers, and ensuring that the kitchen is maintained neatly and kept free of clutter.

- Coordinating with the church office, property committee, or other responsible body the prompt and thorough removal of snow, construction debris, trash, and other hazardous obstacles from church property.

- Scheduling training in first aid for members of the parish.

You should also look for ways to ensure the safety of children on your premises. Most important, you should impose, as a matter of policy, a requirement that children be under adult supervision at all times while on your property. If you have a playground on your premises, you should regularly inspect the equipment for cracks, rust, and other signs of deterioration and make sure that every item is properly anchored. Play should occur in properly designated areas only, not in hallways or the church parking lot.

Finally, there are additional steps to be taken when certain people occupy your premises. When you engage an outside contractor to do repair work, for example, you should take steps to ensure that the contractor will conduct that work with the utmost concern for the safety of your parishioners and other visitors. Ideally, a church official should meet with the contractor before work begins to review the risks involved and plans for minimizing them. If work is being done on the church walls, for example, you should be satisfied that no debris will fall to the ground and injure a passerby. If heavy equipment is being moved onto church property, steps should be taken to ensure that it is not transported while other people are likely to be on-site, and that it is secured while not in use so that children and others do not have access to it. The church should be aware of any dangerous chemicals or other materials the contractor will be using, and the work should be monitored to ensure that procedures outlined at the commencement of the job are adhered to.

2

Liability to Employees

You have a duty of care for your employees that goes beyond their status as invitees. Federal and state governments impose standards of safety on you. Moreover, the employment relationship exposes you to additional risks if you do not treat workers fairly and with respect.

Governmental Workplace Safety Requirements

Have you ever heard of OSHA? Business owners engaged in dangerous activities or handling hazardous chemicals know that the term is an acronym for the Occupational Safety and Health Act, which sets standards for employee safety that they must comply with. The act's provisions are broad enough to cover almost any employer—including churches in certain circumstances—and the standards it sets for certain types of activities are deserving of attention from any employer interested in maintaining a proper work environment.

Though concern for health and safety of workers predates the industrial revolution, federal regulation in this area began only in the middle of the twentieth century, and even then it was limited to specific industries. By 1970, however, concern over persistently high numbers of industrial accidents, coupled with reports of increases in occupational diseases and work-related disabilities, prompted Congress to pass OSHA in an effort to assure a safe and healthful working condition for all employees. Toward that end, OSHA requires all employers covered under its provisions to keep their place of employment free of recognized hazards that are causing or likely to cause death or physical harm. In addition, employers must comply with specific workplace standards that Congress has enacted in areas like training and education, making safety equipment available, and minimizing health hazards.

OSHA applies to any business with employees that affects interstate commerce. Under the Constitution, federal legislation like OSHA can apply only to activities between states, as regulation of purely intrastate commerce is reserved to the states themselves. Within this constraint, Congress intended OSHA to have as broad a reach as permitted by the Constitution, furthering its social purpose of protecting the lives and health of all workers. When do church activities amount to a "business" that affects interstate commerce? Not, Congress has said, when they are purely religious in nature. A fire that breaks out because a candle catches an altar hanging is not within the jurisdiction of an OSHA inspector to criticize.

On the other hand, when a church ventures beyond

spiritual pursuits and enters the secular world, it subjects itself to OSHA's standards and requirements. Schools and day-care centers are clearly "businesses" and are commonly held to be engaged in interstate commerce, even if their students are local, because their books, supplies, and equipment may come from anywhere in the country. This means that a church that runs an educational institution should ensure that the teachers and staff are not subjected to identifiable hazards that may cause death or serious injury, and that standards promulgated under OSHA are complied with. The people who work in the church's thrift shop or bookstore would be entitled to similar protection. Moreover, administrative personnel, such as your office manager, are in theory covered by OSHA, though they do not often engage in the dangerous activities or handle the hazardous substances to which OSHA normally applies.

A church may also be exposed to OSHA sanctions when it hires a contractor to perform repair or remodeling work. If one of the contractor's employees is injured, he or she may sue the contractor for violation of an OSHA safety standard. In such a case, it is a good bet that the church will be sued as well, even though the church relied totally on the contractor's expertise.

OSHA inspectors enforce these edicts through random inspections, though because of limited resources they reach only about one percent of workplaces per year. Even without direct enforcement, however, employers have a strong incentive to voluntarily comply with OSHA's directives, inasmuch as they are designed to promote worker productivity and to help them avoid the devastating effects of a catastrophic accident. A safe working environment is in every church's best interest and promotes good stewardship of the time and talent of your employees.

OSHA has issued voluntary safety and health management guidelines to be used by employers as part of their effort to prevent occupational injuries and illnesses. It developed the guidelines in consultation with safety and health professionals, along with individuals, corporations, professional associations, and labor representatives. The OSHA guidelines recommend that employers adopt a three-part plan to improve occupational safety and health. First, both their management and their employees must commit to protecting workers. Second, work sites should be analyzed so that dangerous situations can be identified and prevented by redesign of the job or the site, or by controlling hazards. Finally, regular training in safety and health needs to be incorporated into regular job practices.

These general principles can be readily transferred to a church environment. First, the pastor and property committee can commit to a program of increased safety and, through communication with the parish as a whole and each member of the staff, develop general enthusiasm for the effort. Second, they can assess the church grounds and buildings, identifying likely hazards and items that need fixing. Is the railing on the balcony loose? How old is the stepladder used by the custodial staff? This is the opportunity to do something about all those low-priority maintenance projects that never seem to get attended to. Finally, the staff can be trained to look for similar potential problems and report them to the property committee as soon as possible. This last point may be the most difficult to institute, as church employees may be reluctant to come forward about potentially dangerous conditions for fear of being labeled a complainer or being blamed for causing them. A program of employee education may be one way to resolve this issue and turn a program of safety and health maintenance into a positive experience.

In addition to prescribing general standards of workplace safety, OSHA provides more detailed guidance with respect to certain particularly common hazards. Much attention in OSHA, for example, is devoted to fire prevention, due to what it terms "a long and tragic history of workplace fires in this country." A number of OSHA's standards in this area deserve attention by church leaders. OSHA mandates, for example, that each workplace have two means of exit that are not near one another and that are never blocked. It requires that buildings be stocked with fire extinguishers of sufficient force that are kept in good working order and that employees be trained to use them. It also dictates that employers have an emergency action plan to facilitate escape and that all employees be trained in what to do if an emergency occurs. Further, OSHA demands that employers create and follow a fire-prevention plan that includes, among other things, procedures for disposing of flammable materials and controlling sources of combustion.

These standards can be adapted for church use. If a procession with candle or torchbearers is part of your liturgy, has someone walked the route recently to make sure that no wall hangings, draperies, or other loose objects can come in contact with the flame? If you have a kitchen on the premises, are steps taken to make sure that the stove is cleaned on a regular basis and that smoke and fire alarms are installed at least in the cooking area if not throughout your premises? Does someone check regularly to make sure that day-care mats or extra chairs are not stored in the vicinity of your fire exits?

These are but a few examples of the creative planning that can result from a review and consideration of OSHA's requirements for all businesses. Further information about OSHA standards is available on the Internet from the OSHA Web site at www.osha.gov. Review and analysis of its basic provisions is a significant effort, but it is one that will pay significant dividends in minimizing the chances of a disastrous accident befalling your valued employees.

Job Discrimination

Other federal regulations restrict the right of an

employer to terminate or discipline workers for discriminatory reasons but most likely do not apply to your church. The Civil Rights Act of 1964 applies only to businesses that "affect commerce" with other states and that employ at least 15 workers for each business day over a period of at least 20 calendar weeks. Churches do not typically "affect commerce" in the course of conducting Sunday services, though if they engage in other activities like administering a school or a retirement home that orders supplies or accepts patients or students from out of state, the required contact with interstate commerce may be found. Such operations may also employ enough workers to meet the 15-employee threshold. Likewise, the 1967 Age Discrimination in Employment Act prohibits discrimination against employees at least 40 years old on account of their age, but it applies only to employers with at least 20 employees that are engaged in a business affecting commerce. Similarly, the more recent Americans with Disabilities Act prohibits employers from refusing to promote, discharging, or otherwise treating unfairly employees with certain physical or mental impairments, but it affects only businesses with at least 15 employees. Most churches, therefore, will be exempt from any federal regulation of their right to discharge employees on any basis they see fit.

In virtually every state, an employer can terminate an employee for any reason or no reason whenever it chooses, unless it has a contractual arrangement with an employee. The contract can be a detailed written document, or it can be as simple as a letter to an employee promising a job for a particular length of time. If you have entered into such an agreement with an employee, you will be bound by the reasonable interpretation of its terms. Moreover, some states do not require a specific agreement to create a contractual arrangement between an employer and an employee limiting the employer's right to fire. A handbook setting forth the policies and practices of the employer and describing the duties involved in a job can establish certain conditions that have to be met before an employee can be let go. Though a disclaimer in the handbook stating that it is not to be read as creating a contractual arrangement with employees will usually suffice to prevent it from acquiring more significance than the employer intended, churches that set forth written regulations for their workers should be sure that they specify that they do not intend thereby to create a contractual arrangement and are not limiting their ability to discharge employees for any reason.

Even though churches face few restrictions on their ability to fire, they should still take a measured approach. Just because a discharged employee will have few grounds on which to challenge the church's action does not mean he or she will not file a lawsuit and try to broker a settlement. Even a church with an excellent case may be forced to incur considerable costs to hire an attorney and file papers to have the matter dismissed.

Time and effort spent before the employee departs to soothe any injured feelings may dissuade him or her from taking matters further.

Minimizing the hardship of a termination starts early in the employment relationship. Employees should have a clear understanding of their job duties and what is expected of them. A job description should be prepared by the appropriate church committee for every employee and updated at least annually as well as every time a new employee begins work. The employee's job performance should be reviewed on a regular basis by the church's personnel committee— which should include both senior clergy and lay leaders—or at least by more people than simply the employee's direct supervisor.

A brief written record of the evaluation should be made, and care should be taken to have the reports be equally detailed for all employees. Being able to show that everyone is treated with equal attention can be very important in dealing with an employee who believes he or she is being singled out. The records and the evaluations should be as specific as possible. Terminating an employee after a few evaluations that have been vague and general will only encourage the perception that the true motivation for the firing was discriminatory or otherwise improper.

How a termination is conducted depends upon the reasons involved. If the employee has not performed up to standard, a record of his or her deficiencies and of efforts to correct them should exist and should be reviewed with the worker. The employee should not be surprised by the decision that has been made. If the discharge is the result of other factors, most notably a lack of funds, the issue becomes more of a pastoral one. The employee's sense of loss and frustration should be acknowledged, and steps should be taken to address his or her legitimate feelings. All efforts to extend benefits, to assist with a job search, and to provide recommendations should be made. A church is, after all, in the business of helping people cope with loss and other problems, and valued employees should be considered to be as much a part of the church family as any member of the congregation.

3

Liability for Actions of Employees and Volunteers

Your employees can expose your church to claims from parishioners and members of the public. Their negligent actions can be imputed to you under certain circumstances. Their failure to supervise others, particularly children, could result in liability being imposed on the church itself. In addition, their intentional conduct can be judged to be your fault if there is sufficient evidence that you failed to thoroughly investigate their background or failed to adequately supervise their conduct while on the job.

Liability for an Employee's Negligent Actions

You can and will be held responsible for the negligence of your employees even though your church did not itself breach any duty of care. An employer is held responsible for harm caused by the negligent actions of its employee under an old doctrine of the law known as "vicarious liability." The theory is that an employer has control over the employee, who was doing the employer's bidding when the accident occurred, and therefore the employer should bear responsibility for the wrong that has occurred. On a more practical level, the justification for vicarious liability is that it is more equitable, or at least more beneficial for the victim, to permit a recovery against a business entity with a connection to the accident than to limit responsibility to an individual who may be able to afford to pay only a fraction of the damages the victim has suffered.

Your "vicarious liability" is limited to the actions of people who are your actual employees. A volunteer who runs his truck into another car while backing out of the church parking lot will not become your legal responsibility. The test of whether someone is your employee is typically stated as whether the person is subject to your control in areas like hours and conditions of work. If you have the right to order the person to work only on certain dates and at certain times, or not to work at all, then the person is probably your employee. The factors that a court is likely to look at include (1) how much skill the job requires, (2) whether you supply materials for the work, (3) whether you pay by the hour, by the job, or in some other way, (4) how long the person has been working, and (5) whether the work being done is church related. Whether the person considers himself or herself to be your employee is also relevant. For these reasons, your minister is probably not an employee of the church. A member of the clergy typically sets his own hours, works without direct supervision, and has rights and responsibilities that are governed at the denominational level.

Even with respect to employees, you can be held responsible for their negligence only if they were acting in the course of their employment. The principal test of whether an employee's actions occurred "in the course" of employment is whether they took place during the employee's normal working hours and in or around the area normally occupied by the employee. This criterion is satisfied if the employee is acting on the instructions of her employer or if he is acting within his express or implied authority by performing normal job functions at the time of the accident. Thus, if an assistant pastor collides with another vehicle while driving to a luncheon with a parishioner, the church will likely be liable for the resulting damages if the pastor is a full-time staff member and usually works during the day. If the accident occurs while he is driving the members of the youth group to an evening concert, your responsibility is less clear since the pastor was working outside of his normal hours and, perhaps, not in pursuit of his normal duties. Finally, if the accident happens while the pastor is on the way to the drugstore on his day off, motivated by a personal desire for toothpaste and not to further church business, the church is unlikely to be implicated.

Failure to Supervise Children

Some courts phrase the issue of "vicarious liability" a little differently, asking whether the injury occurred while the employee was exercising "job-created authority." This is often the question that is raised when a young person is injured during a church-sponsored activity. Where church employees are supervising a group of children on church property during a service or an event you are sponsoring, however, their failure to do so adequately will subject you to liability for any injuries that result. The important question is what is "adequate" supervision, since your employees are not expected to exercise complete control over the children being supervised or be responsible for their own carelessness. Courts usually decide whether the supervision was adequate by considering whether the employees or church officials in charge had specific notice of the dangerous conduct that caused the injury. A spontaneous tussle among the kids being looked after will not give rise to a claim of negligence against the church itself unless church officials were aware that one of them often picked fights and was big and strong enough to inflict injury. Similarly, if a child makes an errant swing during a baseball game at a church social and hits the catcher, the court is unlikely to find the church liable for the injuries unless the batter had a history of causing such accidents and the church did nothing about it

Even if you don't have specific notice of a potential

injury, you can nonetheless be liable for its occurring if a court finds you should have been aware that the children were engaged in an activity that might be hazardous but did not take adequate precautions to protect their safety. Returning to the baseball example, if the errant swing occurred while the kids were playing a pickup game after bats and balls that should have been returned to the equipment area had been left out, and several church officials had noticed that the children were playing but neither stopped to supervise them nor put the equipment away, the church could be held responsible for the resulting injury.

Another way that you can be found liable for failing to properly supervise children is if the environment in which you keep them fails to meet applicable regulations. In Florida, for instance, a church-run day-care center failed to comply with state health department regulations requiring such facilities to provide safe and sanitary outdoor play areas. A child who was bitten by ants while playing outside was allowed to rely upon these regulations, and the church's violation thereof, to establish that the church was negligent to him. This case illustrates that one of the most important things you can do, if you run a day-care center, camp, or school, to protect yourself from liability to the children you are looking after is to comply with all applicable health and safety regulations. Any failure to do so may be accepted by a court as proof, without more, of your negligence and liability to a child in your care.

Another point to take seriously is how you appoint supervisors for activities involving children. Busy parents and a staff spread thin make it difficult to find anyone to chaperone the youth group for an evening of bowling, let alone a weekend camping trip, and it is very tempting to be grateful to anyone who volunteers for the job. It is vitally important, however, that anyone put in a position of responsibility for children be mature and have demonstrated the exercise of sound judgment. It is equally important for that person to have the respect of the youngsters she is in charge of. It is also helpful if she has training in the activity being engaged in and is familiar with the basics of first aid. Also, there is scarcely an activity in which young people engage that a single adult can adequately look after, so having more than one supervisor is a very good idea.

While obtaining a release from parents for liability is probably inadvisable for routine outings involving children because of the suspicions such a document is likely to raise about your confidence in your ability to look after them, it is a good idea to obtain permission from them to take their children on an extended outing. You will also want to get from parents emergency contact information and a list of their child's allergies and past health concerns.

Particular attention should be paid to assigning drivers to transport children to and from church-sponsored activities. It is not out of line to ask for the driving history of potential candidates, even if they are parents of the children involved. If the vehicle being driven is a church-owned van or bus, you must investigate the driver's relevant experience; no one should be learning how to drive an oversized vehicle when the safety of the church's youth is at stake. Drivers should also have demonstrated the ability to assume responsibility and to concentrate in the face of loud noise and other distractions. In addition, rest stops should be scheduled for any lengthy trips as a way to reduce driver fatigue. Every driver should carry a cellular phone for use in the case of breakdown or emergency. Finally, all drivers should have adequate insurance, which should be checked prior to departure, and all vehicles should have an emergency kit including flares and jumper cables.

If the church owns a vehicle in which it transports members of the church or the public, it should make sure to conduct a regular inspection with the aid of a trained professional. This should be supplemented by a pre-drive checklist that is followed whenever the vehicle is used and should include a check of the tires, brakes, mirrors, windshield wipers, lights, and turn signals.

Negligent Hiring

In recent years courts have begun to impose liability on employers and nonprofit organizations when employees intentionally hurt people who are entrusted to their care and the court believes that the employees were not properly supervised or should never have been hired in the first place. Students injured in baseball games have been allowed to sue their school, parents of children who have drowned in a private swimming pool have been permitted to file a claim against the pool owner, and victims of sexual molestation by a co-worker have made claims against their employers, and the common element is that the coach, lifeguard, or employee involved in the incident should never have been hired. In just as many, if not more, cases, however, such averments have been rejected on the principle that schools, employers, and owners are not guarantors of their employees' conduct. The implications of these cases are significant for churches, which often undertake the care of children and other vulnerable people and also reach out, for pastoral reasons, to employ workers whom other employers have rejected because of a colored past or difficulties in complying with societal norms.

In cases where the employee is guilty of mere negligent conduct, a court may find he or she was acting in the scope of his or her employment and may apply the doctrine of vicarious liability to hold the employer responsible. When the employee causes harm intentionally, however, as in the case of a sexual assault, the court is likely to find that the employee was not acting on behalf of his or her employer, and it therefore will be obliged to apply another theory to find liability on the employer's part. In situations where the employer knows or should have known at the time of hiring that some attribute of the employee's character or prior conduct would create an unreasonable risk of harm to those with whom the employee might come into contact in executing his or her employment responsibilities, some courts have determined that the employer's decision to hire the employee, or failure to take any action to prevent the harm, amounts to negligence. These courts have believed it appropriate to hold an employer liable for its negligence in placing an unfit person in a situation where he or she can do harm to others. Often the scope of the investigation a court imposes on an employer is related to the severity of the harm that can be done by the employee whose dangerous propensities go undetected. A church may not fare well under this type of analysis, as the ordinary life of most parishes encompasses a number of activities in which children, the elderly, and other vulnerable groups are entrusted to the care of a single employee.

Two cases from different courts illustrate the application of these rules. One involved a minister who, as a parish assistant, engaged in sexual relations with a female parishioner whom he was counseling. The woman sued not only the minister, but also the diocese by which he was employed, claiming that the affair was responsible for the termination of her marriage and the resurfacing of various mental health problems. It was revealed during the trial that at the time the minister was ordained, he underwent a psychological examination the results of which were given to the diocese and indicated that he suffered from depression and confusion as to his own sexual identity. The woman used this information to argue successfully that the diocese had been negligent in not inquiring further into the minister's capability to counsel parishioners. At a minimum, said the court, the diocese should have conducted an inquiry into whether the minister was capable of counseling individuals and should have informed the vestry of the minister's parish about problems he might encounter with the role he was asked to assume (*Moses v Diocese of Colorado,* 863 P2d 310 [Colo 1993]).

The other case involved a church janitor who forced two boys who happened to be on the premises where he worked into committing acts of oral sodomy. Here, no liability was imposed on the church, because the court found no evidence that it knew or should have known of any prior history by the janitor of such assaults, or of any other aspect of his personality that might suggest it was likely he would commit them (*Moseley v Second New St. Paul Baptist Church,* 534 AQ2d 346 [DC App 1987]).

One key to avoiding liability for negligent hiring or supervision of your employees, then, is in the investigation you conduct during the hiring process. At one extreme, you may decide to ask no questions at all about the background of your prospective employees. This is a risky course, since some courts impose liability on employers if they either knew or should have known about an employee's propensity for misdeeds. Thus, if a telephone call to the prospective worker's previous employer would have elicited the information that the worker was fired for an improper sexual advance, failure to make the call may be regarded as negligence on your part. On the other hand, where you have no basis to suspect a prospective employee has a character defect or is unfit for the job contemplated, you are not required to conduct an investigation worthy of the FBI. As one court said in ruling that a church was not liable for hiring a minister accused of sexually abusing a child: "[W]e do not agree that the Church had a duty specifically to inquire about all of [the minister's] prior sexual conduct in an attempt to ascertain if, for example, he had ever had a homosexual liaison or abused a child." The court held that, given the minister "was apparently a happily married man with a stable family," it was sufficient for the church to determine that he "had no criminal record and had never been arrested or investigated for any crime, sexual or otherwise" (*R.A ex rel. N.A. v First Church of Christ,* 748 A2d 692, 698 [Pa Super 2000]).

Putting the law to one side, however, with respect to employees who will have frequent contact with the public or interaction that will be close and involve a special relationship of trust or care, as a prudent church you should attempt, at the time of hiring, to go beyond what the employee reveals in an interview. At a minimum, candidates for such positions should fill out a written application in which they are asked to summarize their employment history, report and explain any criminal convictions, and supply two or more references. They should also provide proof of identity by means of a driver's license or similar record, along with the addresses of current and previous residences. You can find such application forms at stationery supply stores. Make sure that they include a statement that the candidate must sign certifying that the information he or she is providing is accurate and complete, and acknowledging that any misstatement may be grounds for dismissal.

Then you must contact references and past employers to verify the information that has been reported to you. In the case discussed above, the court was particularly impressed by the fact that the church checked every reference provided to it and no one provided any indication that there was a need for further investigation.

The task of checking references is often undertaken by the minister of the parish because of the need for discretion and the gravity that he or she brings to the task. You should make and keep a written record of each contact in the event a question is raised later as to your efforts to check on the applicant's background. These records should be treated as confidential, by being kept in a secure place to which access is limited. While the person conducting the investigation may share the results with the appropriate persons within the church, such as the personnel committee if one exists, care must be taken not to generally disseminate information about a candidate's background and past activities. If your investigation calls into question any of the information given to you by the applicant, you must discuss the inconsistency with him or her so that it can be resolved to your satisfaction. If it is not, do not make the applicant a job offer.

A criminal background check is also advisable. Convictions, though not necessarily arrests that are dismissed for some reason, are matters of public record in many states and should be available from the local court office for the county or counties in which the applicant has lived. You will need to use discretion in order to weigh the consequences of a candidate's past criminal record, inasmuch as you may determine that rehabilitation and forgiveness are aspects of your outreach and ministry. The nature of the offense, the punishment imposed, the length of time that has passed since the offense was committed, and the candidate's subsequent behavior are among the factors you will want to take into account. Certain types of offenses, however, like child molestation or embezzlement, must be considered grounds for immediate disqualification from positions in which the applicant would be able to commit the same offense once again.

One caution is in order here—a number of states impose restrictions upon the use employers and potential employers can make of information about a person's criminal past. In Pennsylvania, for example, an employer may reject an applicant because of a felony or misdemeanor conviction only if the offense involved is related to his or her suitability for the position in question. You may, for example, decline to hire a convicted child molester as an aide in your day-care center. On the other hand, you could be asking for a lawsuit if you reject the same applicant for a job as a custodian, particularly because, in Pennsylvania, you are obligated to notify him or her in writing if your decision not to offer the position is based even in part on the criminal record you reviewed. It is very important, therefore, that you have up-to-date advice, before you make your next hiring decision, on what criminal background information can be obtained on the applicant in your jurisdiction and what use you may make of that information.

Your church can be held responsible for the conduct of a volunteer as well as an employee if someone is injured because of the volunteer's conduct and it is determined that he or she was unfit for the job assigned. Volunteers should be subjected to the same level of background check as paid employees, which means they must also fill out an application on which they list their experience, deny or affirm past criminal convictions, and provide references. Moreover, it may be tempting to place volunteers into situations for which they are not well suited, such as when a member of a youth group is asked to supervise Sunday school students swimming during a canoe trip. Members of the church should be particularly conscious, therefore, of the possible risk to which they may subject the church by agreeing to take on a responsibility for which they are not qualified, or even by asking someone else to do so. While it is true that the church is responsible only if it knew or should have known of the volunteer's shortcomings, where a lack of experience is obvious for some reason relating to age or physical condition, the volunteer should not be asked to serve.

Negligent Supervision

After you have hired an employee or placed a volunteer, your duty continues to protect the public against any violent or criminal propensities that come to your attention while he or she is working for you. You may hear of such disturbing conduct from another member of your staff who makes a complaint or reports on an employee's actions that he or she finds disturbing. If this occurs, you may be under a duty to make an investigation of the charges unless the person bringing the complaint specifically requests you not to.

Your duty to supervise an employee after he or she is hired extends only to claims brought by people you are obliged to care for. What an employee does on his or her own time is not your responsibility. Also, your duty extends only to conduct that is foreseeable by a reasonable person. If you conduct a thorough investigation of a complaint you receive and determine it is unfounded, you should be relieved of responsibility for the later actions of the same employee, even if they are of a similar type to what was alleged against him previously. You must carefully document your investigation, however, noting in particular the specific charges alleged, the people you spoke with and what they said, the documents involved, and anything else pertinent to your determination that the charges did not warrant action on your part.

Your failure to take such action upon receipt of a complaint is practically a guarantee that you will be sued along with the employee if he or she causes harm to someone at a later date. So is your turning a blind eye to the clear evidence of misconduct or dangerous tendencies that your investigation reveals. Similarly, it is not a good idea to allow an employee you put in the position of taking care of vulnerable members of your parish to do so without any supervision. Teachers can be monitored from time to time during their lessons, drivers should be held to a schedule, and the maintenance staff needs to keep the administrative office informed as to its whereabouts. There are a number of good reasons to supervise your employees that have nothing to do with your potential liability for their conduct, but that possibility provides an additional reason for you to be diligent in your efforts.

A final risk to which you are subject in your role as an employer is that you be sued for defamation by an employee you have terminated. Any discussion, written or oral, that one of your employees has within the church or with any outside person about the termination is capable of being turned into a claim of libel or slander by a fired worker who is disgruntled and looking for retribution. Thus, it is important that you limit or control any such discussion so as to avoid providing ammunition for such a suit.

The disparaging comments may be imputed to the church if made by someone who is facilitating or promoting church business. One court refused to find a church liable for the comments of its minister to legal authorities opining that the church should charge a fund-raiser it hired with misappropriation of church funds. The fund-raiser claimed that the minister's statements were slanderous, but the court ruled that they amounted to no more than his personal evaluation of the fund-raiser's conduct. The fund-raiser failed to demonstrate that when the minister was speaking, he was acting on behalf of the church, because the fund-raiser could not show that one of the minister's job duties was to render personal opinions about members of the congregation. The court concluded that even if the minister's comments were defamatory, there was no way the church could have known or reasonably foreseen he would make them (*Cooper v Grace Baptist Church,* 81 Ohio App 3d 728, 612 NE2d 357 [1992]).

4

Defenses to Liability

A church usually has several defenses available to it against liability claims by members of the public and employees. Depending upon the type of claim being made, you may be able to argue that the plaintiff contributed to his or her own injury or even assumed the risk that it would occur. In addition, other types of claims may be turned away at the outset on the ground that your actions are protected by either the First Amendment of the United States Constitution or the doctrine of charitable immunity.

Comparative Negligence

If you are found to have acted negligently toward a parishioner or member of the public by, for example, failing to repair a broken step outside your sanctuary about which you had notice, you will be held liable for any injury he suffers. The amount of that liability may be mitigated, however, if the court finds that the injured party could have taken steps for his own protection that he did not. For example, if the step was obviously cracked in one section, and the evidence is clear that the victim deliberately stepped in the crack when he could merely have stepped around it, the amount of damages he may be entitled to recover from you could be diminished. If, by contrast, the evidence shows that the crack was concealed to the casual observer or that it ran the length of the step and thus was unavoidable, a judge or jury might conclude that the injured party acted reasonably in walking over it.

Once it is determined that the plaintiff contributed to the accident, a determination must be made as to how to apportion fault. At one time, most jurisdictions followed the rule that a party that was found to have been partly responsible for the injury he or she suffered could not recover at all from a defendant that was also negligent, no matter what their relative responsibility was. Because of the often harsh result this rule produced, states have moved to what is known as the doctrine of "comparative negligence," under which a negligent plaintiff may still recover from a defendant so long as his or her fault is not judged to be greater than the defendant's, but will have the damages reduced by the percentage his or her negligence bears to the total degree of fault. A judge or jury in these types of cases is asked, therefore, to determine what percentage of the total blame for the accident should be assessed to the victim and what percentage to the property owner.

Returning to the example of the broken step, assume that a jury determines that you are 70 percent responsible for the accident because you failed to repair it and the victim who trips and falls on the step is 30 percent responsible for not being more careful about where he walked. If the total amount of his damages were 100,000 dollars, you would be liable for 70,000 dollars under this apportionment. If, by contrast, the victim were found to be 60 percent responsible, you would not have to pay 40,000 dollars. Your dollar liability would be reduced to zero, because under the doctrine of comparative liability a victim cannot recover if his or her fault is determined to be greater than the defendant's.

Assumption of the Risk

There are situations in which an injured party's own negligence is sufficient to relieve a property owner of liability even though the owner is also at fault. Usually this happens when the plaintiff is found to have been aware of a risk created by the defendant's negligence but proceeds voluntarily to encounter it. In such a case a plaintiff may be found to have "assumed the risk," which means he or she had accepted the risk and at least by implication consented to relieve the defendant of its duty. It also comes up when a prospective employee is told that the job for which she is applying may involve exposure to a particular danger—an electrician working with exposed wires, for instance—and takes the job anyway. Assumption of the risk is traditionally distinguished from contributory negligence on the ground that it requires a voluntary, conscious understanding by the injured party of the risk and its apparent consequences, whereas comparative negligence involves a failure to appreciate a risk at the time it is encountered. The consequence of determining that a plaintiff assumed the risk is the same as if the plaintiff is found to be contributorily negligent in excess of 50 percent—the defendant is not liable for any damages.

In the case of a church, assumption of the risk can come up when an employee—perhaps a custodian—notices a defect in a piece of equipment like a ladder but takes the ladder out anyway to change a lightbulb without attempting to either fix the problem or reach the light in a different way. It occurs during the church picnic when someone deliberately sits down in the potential path of foul balls. Only if the person had a free choice to avoid the risk he or she voluntarily encountered, however, can he or she be said to have assumed it. Thus, if you order your custodian to climb to the top of the church tower up a rickety stairway, the custodian will not be held to have assumed the risk of the stairway collapsing while he is on it.

Prohibition on Suits by Parishioners

There is another defense that may be available to you if a person belonging to your church is the claimant. Some states have passed laws prohibiting the members of an unincorporated association like a church from suing the association. Under the law, the members of such an association are considered to be acting jointly in carrying out the association's work, which means that when one is found to be negligent that negligence is applied to all of the other members. This in turn makes a member suing the church for injuries suffered while on church property responsible for her own injuries, and it bars a recovery by such a member against the church.

First Amendment Protection

A court will not determine the liability of a church with respect to certain types of claims because to do so would violate the First Amendment's prohibition on government restrictions on the free exercise of religion. The First Amendment to the U.S. Constitution, which has been applied to the actions of the federal and state courts since the passage of the Fourteenth Amendment, provides that they "shall make no law respecting the establishment of religion, or prohibiting the free exercise thereof." The Supreme Court has construed this amendment to prohibit the "excessive entanglement" of government with religion, such as would occur if a court were required to interpret church law, policies, or practices.

These concerns are raised most notably when a minister sues a church for wrongful termination. One court refused to entertain such a suit on the ground that religious denominations have rules and procedures governing who can become a clergy member and these practices are at least partly based on Scripture or other religious principles with which, the court concluded, the judicial branch of the government should not interfere. To do so, the court held, would be at least indirectly to inject state control over how religious entities conduct their affairs, which is something the First Amendment has been consistently interpreted, for more than 200 years, to prohibit.

For example, it may be that the governing body of the denomination has determined that, in such cases, prayer, counseling, and reflection are the appropriate actions to be taken when a minister has fallen out of touch with his congregation. For a court to order the minister's reinstatement or that damages be paid to him because of the termination would necessarily impact upon the church's own teachings as to the proper resolution of the problem and impede the denomination's ability to deal with the issue in accordance with its scriptural beliefs. The same considerations have been applied to dismiss a defamation claim by a pastoral employee against the church that fired her, the court ruling that

> the First Amendment prevents this Court from scrutinizing the possible interpretations of defendants' statements and their purported reasons for uttering them; to conclude otherwise would effectively thrust this Court into the forbidden role of arbiter of a strictly ecclesiastical dispute over the

suitability of a pastoral employee to perform her designated responsibilities. (*Brazauskas v Fort Wayne-South Bend Diocese,* 714 NE2d 253, 263 [Ind App 1999])

On the other hand, some courts have found claims against ministers arising from alleged sexual misconduct to be permissible under the First Amendment, noting that the Constitution does not provide absolute freedom to act with impunity in the area of religion. Such claims, these courts have reasoned, do not typically require any inquiry into religious doctrine or practice. Rather, as one court put it, "the protection of society requires that religious organizations be held accountable for injuries they cause to third persons" (*Konkle v Henson,* 672 NE2d 450, 456 [Ind App 1996]).

Similarly, claims by third parties who are injured while on church property are typically not subject to a First Amendment defense. The reasoning is that when purely secular conduct is at issue, courts can apply secular standards and hold churches responsible for the effects of their conduct on third parties. The Supreme Court of the United States has characterized this type of analysis as involving the application of "neutral principles" and ruled that the First Amendment does not prohibit such a review of a church's activities. Typically, therefore, when a third person makes a claim against the church, the First Amendment will not provide it with a defense.

Of course, determining when a church's actions are

secular is not always simple. The inquiry leaves a lot of discretion to a court to determine when, for instance, a minister's improper advances to a parishioner are made while he is acting in a religious capacity and when he is on his own time. Comments made while counseling a parishioner, for example, would fall into the former category, whereas the same words uttered during a dinner party probably would not. This is an evolving area of the law, and the prudent church will engage in educational and preventive activities rather than relying upon the First Amendment to relieve it from liability.

Charitable Immunity

The concept that a charitable institution should not have to pay damages for its negligent conduct is long-standing and has been followed in many jurisdictions. While in recent years this principle has been criticized as placing the interests of well-endowed institutions ahead of injured victims, it survives in many places as either a judicial doctrine or a creation of state or local legislatures. If followed in your state, the doctrine of charitable immunity could negate, or at least substantially limit, your liability for some types of damages your church would otherwise be held to account for.

The doctrine of charitable immunity was originally created by judges who were looking for a way to avoid the brutally harsh effect a substantial adverse verdict could have on an institution founded for the public good and lacking substantial financial resources. As far back as the sixteenth century, English courts had opined that trust funds held by a charitable institution could not be used to pay claims against the charity because that was not why the funds were given to the institution. The doctrine never achieved universal acceptance in England, but it was adopted in the United States well over a century ago and eventually was adopted by virtually every state that considered the question.

The principal justification for charitable immunity is that the work of hospitals, orphanages, elder-care facilities, and other charities is of such public importance that they must be protected from having their limited assets dissipated through court proceedings. The theory is that the loss of such funds could render the charity unable to do the good works for which it was created and that the benefit to the public as a whole from such services outweighs the benefit to the individual who would be paid the funds in the form of a judgment.

A related rationale that courts have used to protect charitable assets from liability claims is that the donors who formed the institution in the first place provided it with funds in "trust" for a limited purpose and the trust would be violated if the money was used to pay personal-injury damages. Honoring the intent of the original donors by preserving their funds is judged to promote a more important public purpose than compensating injured victims.

A third theory that is applied in support of immunity is the argument that a person who avails himself or herself of the services of a charity implicitly waives any complaint he or she might have about the quality of services received or about any problem that occurs. For this reason, some courts hold that charitable immunity does not apply when the victim is a stranger, since strangers have accepted no benefit from the charity in return for which they can be said to have waived their right to complain. Interesting questions arise, for example, when the person suing a hospital is the husband of a patient, who is injured by tripping over a broom carelessly left by a hospital employee. The husband does not directly enjoy the hospital's services, but he certainly can be said to benefit indirectly from the care provided his wife. Similarly, does a visitor to your sanctuary who comes to view your stained glass window receive a benefit from his or her visit that warrants absolving you from liability if he or she trips and falls on your stairs on the way out? And why should your liability depend upon whether the injured party is a one-time visitor or a long-standing parishioner?

Since the height of its popularity at the turn of the century, the doctrine of charitable immunity has steadily been eroded, in part because of the difficulties posed by questions like these. Courts have had difficulty reconciling the concept of charitable immunity with the fundamental legal principle that all people are liable for the harm they cause by their careless actions. As one federal court put it, "[W]hether the Good Samaritan rides an ass, a Cadillac, or picks up hitchhikers in a Model T, he must ride with forethought and caution" (*President and Directors of Georgetown College v Hughes,* 130 F2d 810, 813 [DC App 1942]). According to an article in the prestigious *Harvard Law Review,* as of the mid-1980s, 16 states had eliminated the doctrine of sovereign immunity altogether, another 12 refused to apply it to hospitals, and 5 others had abrogated it with respect to institutions other than hospitals. That left 6 states maintaining some form of immunity for all charities, 10 recognizing immunity for hospitals, and 2 applying the doctrine to other types of charities only.

Fundamentally, courts that have refused to apply the charitable immunity doctrine do not believe an innocent victim should be obligated to bear the consequences of any party's negligence. They have viewed the charitable immunity doctrine as an unwarranted exception to the general rule that all people are responsible for the harms they cause and that all victims are entitled to compensation for their injuries. They have pointed out that the notion of a poorly funded charity that will be devastated by having to pay a liability verdict does not comport with the reality that most modern charities are well-endowed and, in any event, can obtain insurance to protect them against the effects of an adverse verdict. It has also been pointed out that for-profit companies are not entrusted by their shareholders with capital for the purpose of paying money to claimants injured by their negligence, but they are nonetheless compelled to do so if they are responsible for the occurrence of an injury.

Other courts had no trouble rejecting the rationale that the beneficiary of a charity has waived any right to complain about injuries she suffers as services are being rendered. They point out that the injured party has in fact made no such bargain with the charity and that simply because the institution is not for profit does not mean that it is entitled to act in a negligent manner with impunity. As one court put it:

> [T]he waiver theory is only fiction. It can have no foundation of fact in many cases. It cannot be said that a patient taken to a hospital in an unconscious condition knowingly waived the right to recover for negligence that might occur while the patient is unconscious. Neither can it be said that a small child in attending a church service knowingly waived the right to recover for negligence. (*Foster v Roman Catholic Diocese of Vermont,* 70 A2d 230, 235 [Vt 1950])

Another issue that has arisen is the severity of the offenses for which immunity is sought. A century ago, when charitable immunity was at its height of popularity, the typical injury for which compensation against a nonprofit institution was sought was caused by a slip and fall on church property. Today, not only have automobiles added a whole new dimension to the claims that may be brought, but the advent of claims for sexual misconduct has dramatically increased the potential liability to which churches may be subjected. There is substantial public pressure, to which courts are not completely immune, to hold churches and their ministers accountable for such conduct, and a corresponding unwillingness to grant blanket immunity in such situations.

Similarly, the concept of a charity as a small institution existing hand-to-mouth, utterly dependent on the benevolence of its patrons and constantly facing financial hardship, has changed. As one court put it,

> [C]haritable enterprises are no longer housed in ramshackly wooden structures. They are not mere storm shelters to succor the traveler and temporarily refuge those stricken in a common disaster. (*Flagiello v Pennsylvania Hospital,* 417 Pa 486, 493 [1965])

Many receive substantial public funding, whether through tax breaks, admission fees, or, as in the case of hospitals, direct fees for service. While most churches are not in this category, courts generally have not seen fit to exempt them from the broad liability they have generally imposed on charitable institutions.

In Pennsylvania, for example, the Supreme Court first eradicated the principle of charitable immunity in 1965 with respect to hospitals. The main argument it advanced for doing so was that hospitals had become sizable businesses with primarily paying clientele, and it was no longer appropriate to exempt them from liability because of some perceived need to shelter their assets for the common good. Two years later, when presented with a claim by a person who fell on the sidewalk outside a synagogue, the same court extended its previous decision and lifted the exemption with respect to all charities. It concluded that to draw a distinction between paying supporters of an institution and other beneficiaries of its services had no basis under the law. The court said:

> Were such a conclusion to be reached, we might be required to hold that in cases such as the one at bar involving a religious institution, that a dues-paying member of the congregation could recover while another person not so situated could not. (*Nolan v Tifereth Israel Synagogue,* 425 Pa 106, 109 [1967])

As you can well imagine, charitable institutions did not take the eradication of their immunity lying down. Faced with increasing lack of sympathy in the courts, they turned to a body with the power to restore their exemption: state legislatures. Today, a hodgepodge of regulations have been enacted across the country, as each state has taken a slightly different approach to the question of whether, and under what circumstances, a nonprofit institution may avoid liability for wrongful conduct.

In New Jersey, the interplay between the legislature

and the judiciary on this issue has been particularly pointed. Through the first half of the twentieth century, New Jersey courts held that charities were immune from liability to anyone who could be identified as a beneficiary of their services, including girl scouts injured while attending a scout meeting in a church and a student at a parochial school injured by a fellow student. People deemed not to be beneficiaries, such as a guest at a church social event or a driver injured by a church van that skidded off the road, were not prohibited from recovering against a nonprofit entity liable for their injuries. This distinction led to substantial debate as to who qualified as a beneficiary. In one leading case from the mid-1950s, a surgeon on the staff of the hospital where he was injured in an elevator accident was deemed not to be a beneficiary of the hospital and therefore was allowed to bring suit against it. The hospital argued that the surgeon received a tremendous benefit by being associated with it, but the court found the relationship was mutual, in that the surgeon had achieved a state of prominence in his field and, of course, earned money for the hospital through his professional work. Under this view of the law, the pastor of a church would similarly not have been deemed a beneficiary, as he would likely have been found to be rendering financial and spiritual services to the church in return for his salary.

Then, in 1958, the New Jersey Supreme Court declared that charities would no longer be able to claim immunity for their wrongful acts, holding that

> due care is to be expected of all, and when an orga-
> nization's negligent conduct injures another there
> should, in all justice and equity, be a basis for
> recovery without regard to whether the defendant
> is a private charity. (*Collopy v Newark Eye & Ear
> Infirmary*, 27 NJ 29, 39 [1958])

On the same day, the court allowed a case involving a parishioner who fell in a church vestibule while attending mass to proceed to trial, making clear that its repudiation of the doctrine of charitable immunity was not limited to hospitals. Less than two months later, the state legislature passed a law reinstating immunity for all nonprofit institutions "organized exclusively for religious, charitable, educational or hospital purposes" against claims of negligence by any beneficiary of the institution's services, putting courts right back in the business of determining who is and is not a "beneficiary" of the charity's services. Originally, the statute was to have expired after a year, its purpose being to afford charities a period of time to safeguard property and obtain insurance before suits against them would commence. It was renewed after 12 months, however, and remains in effect today.

Here are some examples of how the doctrine of charitable immunity has been applied. Courts have held that a guest at a wedding ceremony at the church benefited from the social function being performed. The court held that "in providing the site of the ceremony the church contributed the preservation of moral or sociological concepts held by the community generally" (*Rupp v Brookdale Baptist Church,* 2442 NJ Super 457, 463 [1990]). A similar result was reached in cases of a guest attending an annual festival, ruling that the function promoted the church's ethnic traditions in accordance with the purposes for which it was founded. Another court held that a woman who was injured while picking her son up from a church-sponsored school could not sue the church because she was on the premises in an effort to further her objective of obtaining a religious-based education for her child. Noting that a statutory intent to promote immunity should be broadly supported, the court concluded that the woman was under the church's beneficence at the time she was injured, and thereby barred from raising her claim. In another case, a church elder was injured when she was driving past the church, noticed that an electrician with whom she needed to discuss some matters was inside, and fell as she was entering the building. The court concluded that the immunity statute "clearly immunizes a charitable organization from the tort claim of a member of the organization who has been injured while working as a volunteer for its benefit" (*George v First United Presbyterian Church,* 272 NJ Super 294, 296 [1984]).

In some states, directors and officers of nonprofit institutions are immune from liability. In others, volunteers cannot be sued. Without immunity, the difficulties in recruiting people to volunteer their time and effort to running and doing the work of a charitable institution would be greatly compounded, as potential workers would decline to become involved because of fears of being sued. Other states take a more restrictive approach to charitable immunity. In Massachusetts, for example, persons injured by a nonprofit's negligent conduct are free to sue the organization, but they can recover no more than 20,000 dollars if the wrongful conduct was performed to carry on the church's charitable purposes. Commercial activities, defined in the Massachusetts statute as those "carried on to obtain revenue," are excluded from this cap even if the revenue is designed "to be used for charitable purposes." Thus, a visitor to a church fair may be free to sue for injuries he suffers there without regard to the 20,000 dollars limitation imposed by the Massachusetts statute. Conversely, however, one Massachusetts court held that a church could allow its parishioner to use a meeting room for a private function and maintain immunity when one of the guests is injured. It determined that what the church did was a natural outgrowth of its original charter to spread moral and religious knowledge, and not in furtherance of a commercial enterprise.

Similarly, Texas caps the liability of a charitable organization other than a hospital, but at the more Texas-like size of one million dollars for a single occurrence. Texas also follows another growing trend by providing immunity for a volunteer who causes death, damage, or injury while in the service of a charitable organization, provided he is "acting in good faith and in the course and scope of his duties or functions within the organization" and the organization itself carries liability insurance and thus has resources to pay any claim that may be attributable to it. The legislature noted that it passed this law—known as a "Good Samaritan statute"—because, in part, the willingness of volunteers to offer their services to charitable organizations "is deterred by the perception of personal liability arising out of the services rendered to these organizations," and "because of these concerns over personal liability, volunteers are withdrawing from services in all capacities." Rhode Island has enacted a similar statute but has determined that the immunity will not apply if the volunteer's conduct is "malicious, willful or wanton," or if he is operating a motor vehicle.

Finally, you should remember that even in states that continue to adhere to the doctrine of charitable immunity, your church is not likely to be able to invoke it for injuries caused while it is engaged in a profit-making activity. Thus, if someone falls at your annual fair or during weekly bingo night in your basement, they are likely to be entitled to sue you even if your state recognizes some form of exemption for nonprofit groups.

5

Insurance

Obtaining proper and adequate insurance coverage for potential liabilities is an important part of any church's strategy for protecting against them. Insurance companies will offer protection for your negligent conduct, and even certain types of intentional acts, for a fee known as a "premium." You will usually be provided such insurance along with the policy that protects you against damage to your property from fire and other causes. The liability coverage you will be afforded contains technical insurance language, along with exclusions and definitions with which you are probably unfamiliar. Most insurers use the same provisions, so certain generalizations may be made about the coverage you should receive.

Most liability insurance policies are effective for a one-year period, and the date on which they begin and end should be prominently set forth. Shorter or longer periods are possible, and you are entitled to change companies at any time. An insurance company is likewise free to decline to renew its agreement with you upon expiration. It may not have the same liberty, however, to cancel you in the middle of a policy term. Many states impose limitations on an insurer's right to drop an insured before the end of the period specified in the policy, so that the insured is not suddenly left without coverage, and require the insurer to notify you of its intention to cancel. Someone on your safety committee or office staff should be in charge of making sure your liability insurance policy is kept up to date and that premiums are paid on time.

Every insurance policy states the maximum amount of indemnity it will provide during the period it is in force, which is known as the "aggregate limit" of coverage. There is a direct relationship between the amount of coverage provided and the amount of premium you pay, but most insurers will not go above a certain limit regardless of how much you are willing to purchase. For most types of liability coverage, there is no point in securing less than one million dollars per year, since in these litigious times even the most routine slip-and-fall case exposes you to an award of that magnitude and since there is no guarantee that you will not have two or even more claims made against you in a given year. Many policies also impose a "per occurrence" limit, which specifies the maximum the insurer will pay on an individual claim no matter how much is left in the aggregate.

The insurance policy you receive will most likely include a number of pages. At or near the front will be the "declarations page," which sets forth the policy term, the types of coverage provided, and the monetary limits. This page is updated when the new policy period commences and is your best evidence as to exactly what coverage you have been given. The declarations page will also make reference to certain policy forms that provide the basic coverage and to additional forms, called "endorsements," that modify the standard forms in specific ways.

The standard commercial liability coverage form issued by most insurers indemnifies you against sums you are legally obligated to pay as damages because of bodily injury or property damage to which the insurance applies. Bodily injury includes sicknesses, diseases, and even death as well as physical harm, and property damage means physical injury to tangible property as well as loss of use of such property. For the insurance to apply, the bodily injury or property damage must result from an "occurrence" that took place while the policy was in effect. An occurrence is usually defined to include "an accident, including continuous or repeated exposure to substantially the same general conditions." It is the date of the occurrence, not the date you are sued, that dictates whether a policy must respond to a claim. If, for example, you have Policy A running from January 1 to December 31 of Year 1, and Policy B covering January 1 to December 31 of Year 2, and a passerby falls on your steps and injures herself on June 1 of Year 1, it is Policy A that will cover her claim whether she files suit in Year 1 or Year 2.

The liability insurance policy will have certain exclusions of which you should be aware. Most notably, you cannot insure against occurrences that you either intended or expected to occur. Accidents that occur on your premises will not usually fall into either of these categories, though if you have a potentially dangerous situation that you are fully familiar with yet take no steps to correct for a substantial period of time, a court may conclude that you expected any harm that is attributable to it. You will also not have coverage for any injuries that result from intoxication that you caused or contributed to, which is a point to remember if you serve alcoholic beverages at any functions you sponsor. You will also not be covered for liability to an employee for work-related injuries, which is why it is important that you maintain workers' compensation coverage for such situations.

Along with the responsibility to indemnify you against any liability imposed upon you as the result of a covered claim, your liability policy imposes upon your insurer the responsibility to defend you against the claim. This usually means that your insurer will find you an attorney and pay his or her bills directly. It will also pick up the related costs of any lawsuit, such as court filing fees and expenses for court reporting services. If you have an attorney you use regularly, you may be able to convince the insurance company to allow him or her to represent you, but ordinarily it will want to select someone with whom it is familiar or that does work exclusively on its behalf.

Remember that by ceding control of your case to

your insurer, you are also leaving the question of settlement in its hands. While the insurer may consult with you on the subject, since it is footing the cost of the case the question of how and when to terminate the suit is in its hands. This can be an issue if you believe the case against you is without merit, but the insurance company settles anyway because it is concerned about the costs associated with preparing the case for trial. The insurance company may pay the claimant to terminate his or her lawsuit whether you believe doing so is a good idea or not.

One very important provision of your general liability policy concerns your obligation to notify your insurer of a potential claim. The insurance policy is likely to say that you must give notice "as soon as practicable" of an occurrence or event that might give rise to a claim. Obviously, you can inform the insurance company only about events that you yourself have learned about, but on its face this provision nonetheless appears to impose quite a significant burden. If your minister notices an elderly man stumble on the sidewalk outside your church, must he contact your insurer to report the event on the chance the passerby might someday claim to have had a heart attack caused directly by your negligent maintenance of your premises? A significant amount of time and resources could be dedicated toward satisfying this obligation. For this reason, courts in most states have established that an insurer cannot refuse to provide coverage for a claim on the ground it did not receive notice in a timely fashion unless it can demonstrate it was prejudiced by not hearing about the claim more promptly. An insurer can rarely show prejudice unless so much time has gone by that witnesses have moved or evidence has disappeared. Nonetheless, it is important that you promptly notify your insurer when you receive any legal papers indicating a claim has either been made or threatened against you, and there is nothing wrong with advising your insurer about any significant accidents or other developments that you think might give rise to a lawsuit.

The insurance policy you obtain probably includes information as to how you should report a claim and to whom. You may be given a form with your policy that you are to use to report potential incidents. Once you submit a claim, the insurance company will notify you as to whether it believes the claim is covered by its policy. If the insurance company reports no coverage, you can attempt to persuade it otherwise. Your ultimate remedy is a lawsuit against the insurance company for what is called a "declaratory judgment," which is an order from the court directing the insurance company to defend and indemnify you against the incident in question.

Frequently you will be able to obtain insurance through a program established by your denomination. Episcopal churches in the same diocese, for example, are often insured through a program established with a single insurer. An insurance company typically saves money by insuring a large group of similar risks, and it can pass those savings on to you, making insurance under a group plan less expensive for you than if you were to obtain it in the open market. You will want to be sure that the company you engage is financially sound, since you are counting on it to be around to pay claims not just when it issues your policy but several years later as well. Several periodicals report the financial strength of insurance companies, and one or more should be consulted by you before you make a final decision. The insurance company will likely have a broker in your area who will arrange for your property to be evaluated and answer any questions that you have. It is of paramount importance that you be able to establish a rapport with your agent since you will rely on your agent for sound advice as to how much and what kind of coverage you need and how to respond to claims against you.

Your general liability policy will also cover you for damages that fall within the policy's definition of "personal injury," which include libel and slander claims made against you along with injuries allegedly caused by your minister while he is acting as a counselor, or by another person acting at the minister's direction. The counseling liability provision will not apply if the minister is acting dishonestly or fraudulently or if the minister charges for the advice he gives.

A popular endorsement to the general liability policy covers claims for sexual misconduct that results in bodily injury, mental anguish, or emotional distress. Such claims may not be covered by the general policy because the law does not recognize mental anguish and emotional distress as "bodily injuries" to which the policy would apply. The sexual misconduct endorsement typically covers not just your church, but also your employees, volunteers, and directors, provided they are acting within the scope of their duties. It usually excludes, however, any person who participates in misconduct or knowingly permits it to occur. The insurance company that issues this type of endorsement will also handle the defense of sexual misconduct claims.

Another type of endorsement about which you should inquire covers your directors, officers, and trustees against errors or misstatements they make in their official capacity, along with failures or breaches of their duties. These days it is not uncommon for parties suing for injuries resulting from defects in premises to claim not just that the property owner failed to take proper care of its building and grounds, but also that its directors acted wrongly in not establishing a procedure under which such problems could be detected and rectified. Similarly, as we have seen, people who contend a church employee sexually abused them frequently argue that the employee should never have been hired and that church officials acted wrongfully in failing to investigate the employee's past. Because of these and other such cases, many of the best-qualified church leaders will refuse to serve unless they are assured of being protected, through a director's and officer's policy, from claims of misconduct while in office. Such a policy typically excludes claims for bodily injury and therefore is limited to amounts you are required to pay on behalf of your directors for an error, misstatement, misleading statement, or omission.

Conclusion

You should not come to the end of this book with feelings of dread and trepidation about the work to be done to make your church free from risk. Such a project will never succeed, as it is impossible to completely insulate any property from danger and not something you should even want to try. A church should strive to be open and inviting and to bring people closer to God. Protecting a church like a fortress, or restricting access, will hinder the achievement of these primary goals.

You can, however, be welcoming and prudent at the same time. Everyone in your parish, for instance, should be responsible for reporting any hazardous conditions or defects to a designated person, perhaps a minister, lay leader, or office director. All members of your community can contribute to reducing the possibility of accidents on your property, and they should regularly be reminded of their responsibility at meetings and through your newsletters and service bulletins.

In addition, you can make great strides toward minimizing your chances of being sued simply by acting promptly to address problems as you learn of them. Too often maintenance and repairs are put off. The problem may not be communicated to the person responsible for fixing it. Calls to outside contractors are deferred, and follow-up inspections by busy clergy and lay personnel are not made. Establishing clear lines of authority and a process for repair and review of defective conditions should be an essential aspect of your property management program.

Finally, make sure that your insurance policy is complete and up to date. Even more important, make sure that you understand what it includes and excludes. Many insurance brokers have considerable experience in dealing with churches and will be happy to explain the policy provisions to your leaders and answer their questions.

By maintaining your property, you create a welcoming atmosphere for regular congregants, guests, and prospective new members. You also act as faithful stewards of God's gifts to you. It may seem time-consuming and not particularly spiritual, but it is among the most important work you are entrusted to do.